Wedding
p l a n n i n g

CONTRACT NEGOTIATION

Save Money, Reduce Stress, and

Have the Wedding You Desire

By Sue Shafer

FOREWORD
by Marsha Lichtenstein

When my husband, Jeff, and I married in July 2000, we decided to have a do-it-yourself wedding and to hold it at our home. It was the second marriage, and second wedding, for each of us. We decided to have a low-key party instead of a formal event.

We did a good job, working together on a plan and meeting with potential caterers, florists, and providers of tables and chairs for the backyard, and other vendors whose services we needed. Even with putting our two heads together, however, we ended up with a serious miscommunication with the florist who presented us with a bridal bouquet of flowers that were the wrong color and wilted! Some of the mistakes were entirely in our own hands, however. I remember we left our beautiful wedding cake sitting inside the steamy house while the party took place outdoors. When we went to find it, the chocolate frosting was already melting and sliding down the sides of the cake. We had not remembered to assign someone to cake duty!

In this book, Sue Shafer walks you through everything you need to know to negotiate professionally with the people who will help make your wedding day smooth, flawless and relaxed. Best of all, as you and your spouse-to-be navigate the dance of negotiation with vendors, you will gain important skills that you will use over and over during your marriage, when you buy a home, plan vacations, and enjoy holidays with extended family.

As I frequently remind my clients, everything is negotiable. And Sue drives this point home in these clear, illustrative and helpful chapters. Here are some excellent suggestions and tips from this book:

Don't buy into the "culture trap" of assuming that wedding service providers won't negotiate with you. The first time you hear the costs and pricing, there's no need to take them at face value. They are starting points for your negotiation.

Understand which services are most easily negotiated and spend your time and energy negotiating with the providers of those services.

Don't be afraid to negotiate: women are often intimidated by negotiation because they imagine it is the same as conflict. Actually, a good negotiation is a conversation between you and the vendor, where together you are going to get to the best combination of services and prices that work for both of you.

Decide what is most important for you to have on your wedding day and be willing to be flexible about the less important niceties, so you can be prepared to have a successful negotiation conversation.

As Susan points out, when you work together to create an affordable wedding with the most important bells and whistles you want for that special day, you and your future spouse establish a model and mindset that carries forward into your marriage. You will continue to work together to get the best prices and best deals for most of your big household purchases – for example, – buying a car, getting the best price on a washing machine, negotiating away the delivery charges for a bedroom – a collaboration you began during the time you were planning your wedding.

So whether you are having an elegant formal affair or a relaxed, do-it-yourself celebration in your backyard, this book is guaranteed to help you feel more comfortable and confident speaking up and asking for what you want as you plan your wedding day.

In my opinion, it is "required reading" for all engaged couples.

Marsha Lichtenstein, Ph.D.
President, Women in Negotiation
Albuquerque, NM

Table *of* Contents

INTRODUCTION

Your beloved planned a very special day. Maybe it involved all of your favorite activities. Maybe you were surrounded by friends, family, and loved ones. Maybe you were whisked away to a romantic location, wooed with delicious food and expensive champagne. Perhaps you were surprised when your special someone bent to one knee. Perhaps you saw it coming.

Regardless of the details, the moment that sparkly, beautiful, love-proclaiming ring slipped onto your finger, your dreams turned into a swiftly approaching reality. When you and your loved one are engaged to be married, it's easy to get caught up in the fantasy of a big, white wedding, a day filled with laughter, tears, and proclamations of love, and endless visions of wedded bliss. In those brief moments after the question has been popped and the answer given, your thoughts are focused on the big picture, and the intricate details of planning a wedding are distant and unimportant.

It doesn't take long, though, for reality to catch up with your rapidly beating heart. Does it? For many couples, planning a wedding is one of the three most stressful experiences they will encounter throughout their married lives. Along with purchasing a home and having a child, no other event promises more late nights, frantic hair-pulling, worries about finances and budget requirements, and general chaos. Let's face it: planning a wedding can be a headache, but there are solutions other than aspirin that can help to relieve some of the pressure.

There are thousands of resources for couples that can assist in the wedding planning process, and for a basic rundown of the myriad tasks associated with a wedding ceremony, I invite you to explore my first book in this series, Wedding Planning: Ask These Questions to Avoid Costly and Upsetting Problems. It's a great tool that will help engaged couples navigate the process of hiring photographers, wedding coordinators, facilities and caterers and purchasing things like wedding gowns, bridesmaid dresses, tuxedos, and even that all-important cake.

This book, the second in the series, is quite a different tool. Most engaged couples are aware that they'll be expected to share a first dance on the eve of their wedding. What they fail to realize, though, is that this isn't their first dance at all. The wedding planning process involves a very complicated, relatively unknown, and indescribably crucial dance: one in which many couples never even realize they are participating.

This is the dance of negotiation.

As brides- and grooms-to-be meet with wedding service providers, they'll be bobbing and weaving to the dance of negotiation. Negotiation is an inescapable part of modern human life, and yet it's a part for which many people are ill-prepared. This book aims to fix that problem by providing invaluable information about wedding contract negotiation. By exploring the concept of negotiation, starting with its history and moving forward into modern negotiation tactics, addressing the issues that many women face when it comes to negotiation, and detailing various tactics, tips, and tricks that couples can use, the overall cost of a wedding can be dramatically lowered even while soon-to-be-married couples create the truly perfect wedding.

Why is negotiation such a "hush hush" subject in today's modern world? Why are so many people afraid to banter and barter when it comes to service and product costs? Why are we hopelessly unprepared when it comes to stating our needs and our budget and seeking to fulfill both?

We often treat negotiation like a thing of the past. An engaged woman may listen patiently to a photographer explain his or her pricing structure and available options and mistakenly believe that there is no room to wiggle. On the contrary, wedding service providers are often quite willing to make adjustments, offer additional services, and accommodate restrictive wedding budgets.

"This is great," you say to yourself, "but how do I get the best services at the lowest prices? What's the magic word?"

Alas, if it were that easy this book would consist of a single page, and the world would be forever changed. Negotiation can be convoluted and complicated. It can be stressful and even terrifying. Mistakes in negotiation can cause serious problems including burned bridges, frustrated service providers, wasted money, and services that don't meet a couple's standards or expectations.

That's why we call it a dance.

Just like any dance, though, the art of negotiation can be taught. It can be learned. The steps can be practiced and rehearsed, an individual can improve over time, and negotiation can turn from an elusive idea into a comfortable and profitable behavior.

Are you ready to learn the ins and outs of negotiation? Are you ready to sit down with a potential wedding service provider armed with the ability to communicate effectively, confidently, and successfully? Do you want to save money on your wedding, creating the ceremony of your dreams without pushing your stress levels to the maximum?

Wedding Planning: Contract Negotiation is going to help you. In this book you'll find research-backed facts about effective negotiation strategy and tactics paired with example stories that illustrate these tactics being put into good use. You'll find advice from authoritative, brilliant negotiators like Marsha Lichtenstein of WomenNegotiate.com, Linda Babcock and Sara Laschever, authors of Ask For It, and several others.

Remember: don't let yourself get overwhelmed by the prospect of negotiating contracts. That is the opposite effect this book is intended to have. It's easy to assume that negotiations are too daunting for the layperson, too sophisticated for an inexperienced negotiator. This couldn't be further from the truth! Anyone can learn to negotiate. If you feel yourself getting overwhelmed, take a break. Make an entry in a personal journal, or use the back pages of this book to jot down your thoughts and concerns. Spend some time filling out the included worksheets. These resources will help you approach negotiation in a methodical, step-by-step way that's far less stressful than simply jumping in head first.

Planning your wedding doesn't have to give you worry lines. Leave that to your future children. Ready to learn an invaluable lesson on negotiation?

Let's get started.

Chapter 1
HISTORY of HAGGLING

5-Hour Energy, an energy-boosting product sold in small bottles, recently started offering its product in six-pack packaging. To advertise this new move, they created a comical commercial that has attracted a lot of consumer attention. In the commercial, a female shopper places six individual bottles of the beverage on the conveyor belt in the checkout lane. She's shopping in a standard grocery store or convenience store, and the clerk mechanically swipes her purchases across the scanner and recites the price to the eager shopper.

Then, things get a little strange. Instead of handing over cash for the purchase, the lady decides to haggle. She offers a lower price for the product. The clerk is, needless to say, quite surprised. She laughs at the audacity of the female shopper and proclaims, "No ma'am, we don't haggle here." Undeterred, the woman offers another possible price. The clerk's humor quickly turns into frustration. The commercial ends when the clerk suggests that the shopper buy the six-pack variety in order to save, since the haggling is clearly not going to work.

Why is this commercial so funny? The ad works because our modern culture recognizes the ridiculousness of trying to haggle pricing in a major grocery store chain. This is just something we don't do. Have you ever walked into Starbucks, ordered a latte, and then offered to pay 25 cents less than the price on the sign? Of course you haven't! We inherently know that anyone who tries to save money through that route is going to walk out of Starbucks without a latte.

Ed Brodow is a negotiation expert. In fact, the chairman of the United States Securities and Exchange Commission, Harvey Pitt, once called Brodow the "King of Negotiation." Brodow's experience in the art of negotiation has led him to conduct extensive training seminars with big-time earners and high-profile individuals including employees at Microsoft and even government workers. He explains the general lack of negotiation skills quite succinctly by saying that modern humans simply do not possess a "negotiation consciousness."

Translation: we fail to view the majority of commercial interactions as a negotiation. Negotiation is no longer a part of our programming. It's not something we do on a regular basis. It's not a set of skills that we expect to need in our lives. Sure, we still engage in minor negotiations on a semi-regular basis. Have you ever tried to decide on a restaurant with a group of friends? Everyone states their case for bringing the group to a favorite establishment, the pros and cons of the situation are weighed, and a decision is made. This is a type of negotiation, and we do encounter situations like this pretty regularly.

However, when it comes to, say, buying a television set, purchasing an automobile, or even paying for a wedding cake, many people clam up and willingly pay the first price they are quoted. Why do we do this? Why don't we haggle like the woman at the grocery store in the 5-Hour Energy commercial?

Where has our "negotiation consciousness" gone?

To understand this very basic problem, we need to look to history.

History of Bartering, Haggling, and Negotiating

It may be hard to believe, but the drift away from negotiation as a standard of life is actually quite recent when compared to the history of commerce amongst human beings. This drift can be partly explained by the introduction of currency into our modern society. Let's take a look at a humorous story:

Hundreds of years ago, a man named Clump lived with his family in a mud hut. His family was part of a larger village, and the community lived in relative peace. Clump was a sheep farmer. He had a flock of healthy, beautiful sheep, and he spent every day tending to that flock of sheep. When it came to thick, woolen clothing, fresh sheep's milk, and roasted mutton, Clump's family was all set. These things, though, didn't cover all of Clump's family's basic human needs. What about pots for cooking mutton stew? Tools for butchering and skinning sheep? Weapons to protect against wolves?

For those things, Clump needed to visit the mud hut next door. Grump was a blacksmith. He lived alone, and he spent his days stoking a fire and working lumps of raw iron into usable tools. Grump had knives, spears, scythes, shields, armor, pots, cooking utensils, and hundreds of other iron tools at his disposable. However, Grump didn't have anything to eat. His blacksmithing work took up too much time to manage a flock of sheep. What was he to do? Luckily, his neighbor Clump had an idea.

Clump could offer extra wool and meat to Grump in exchange for some iron tools. This arrangement sounded great, but how were the two men to come to an agreement? There were no iPhone apps that converted sheep into iron tools. There was no daily exchange ticker to help with currency conversion.

In order to make a fair trade, a discussion took place. Grump showed Clump how difficult it was to make iron tools. He showed him how many tools he had in his collection and the time required to make a single tool. Clump gave Grump a tour of his fields. They counted sheep, talked about the difficulties involved in a shepherd's daily life, and came to an agreement.

There was no paper money, no coins, no checks, and certainly no credit arrangement. In an agrarian society, like the Clump's and Grump's, haggling was simply a necessity. There was no other way to exchange goods and services than by haggling or trading. While this concept is foreign to us, we still use the word "trade" today. When you meet a new acquaintance, you might ask him or her what "trade" they are in. This concept of trading one good or service for another still permeates our "sophisticated" culture.

Even so, it's easy to see why negotiation has "faded from our consciousness," as Brodow puts it. Nobody today pays for their wedding cake in sheep. You're not going to meet with a photographer to discuss how many chicken eggs he wants in exchange for four hours of work and 500 photos. Instead, we deal in currency—paper and metal that's backed by a regulated treasury. Even without getting into the details of modern commerce, it's easy to see why haggling disappeared. We view money has having an intrinsic value. You know how much a dollar is worth to you. You have a basic understanding of what $100 can buy in today's society. Because there is no reason to have a conversation about the value of your money, you start to trust that stores are offering goods and services at the best value possible.

We accept prices at face value, and it feels strange to question
14

the price of a product. A television costs a certain amount to manufacture, and this manufacturing cost is passed onto the consumer. Quid pro quo. Tit for tat. Arguing the price of an energy drink is laughable, and we accept this.

This mindset gets us into trouble, though, especially when it comes to purchasing services. Services are more fluid and subjective than products. A latte costs $4 because when you add up the cost of milk, coffee, flavors, and the cup in which it is served, it comes close to $4. With wedding services like photography, wedding coordination, transportation, etc. this addition formula doesn't really work.

How much is time worth? What is the value of experience? How much should one charge for quality? Craftsmanship? Superior tools? Customer service? Dedication? Friendliness?

You see the problem. For many couples, the solution to this problem of pricing and valuing services eludes them. Clump and Grump, though, know the answer: negotiation. A conversation about value, a discussion about needs and desires, a question or two about the service in question can clear up the ambiguity surrounding service cost and value. Maybe our "thick-skulled" ancestors knew a thing or two that we've forgotten.

Anticipating the Culture of Negotiation

Negotiation can help you understand the cost of basic wedding services, and it promotes positive communication between a couple-to-be and their service providers, but it can also help you avoid something I like to call the "Negotiation Culture Trap." That's an ominous term, but it's actually a very simple concept. To understand the culture trap of negotiation, let's consider an example.

Stephanie was planning a month-long trip to Europe after her college graduation. Because she'd never travelled worldwide, she booked the trip through a travel agency. This agency set her up with guided tours in every city on her schedule. Her first stop was Paris, France. Before disembarking from the tour bus, her tour guide made an announcement.

"Listen up, people. You'll find lots of street vendors and artists on the Parisian streets. Remember: no matter what you do, never pay the asking price. Always offer less."

This seemed rather heartless to Stephanie, so when she discovered a beautiful watercolor painting by an old Frenchman in the heart of the city and was told the price was 150 euros, she gladly paid the asking price. After all, this man worked hard on the painting, and he deserved a fair wage.

When she returned to the bus, another traveler, Dennis, revealed to Stephanie that he had purchased the exact same painting at half the cost!

How strange, thought Stephanie. If the artist was willing to sell the painting for 75 euros, why on earth did he ask 150 euros to begin with?

The answer is the Negotiation Culture Trap. It's most clearly seen in the sale of souvenirs to tourists, but this scenario occurs in thousands of businesses around the world. What Stephanie didn't realize was that the artist expected her to haggle with him. After dealing with thousands and thousands of tourists trying to get the best possible price, this artist realized that asking for a higher amount upfront would allow him to sell paintings at a rate that would sustain his business.

Over time, the artist developed a culture of negotiation. In his mind, negotiation was to be expected. In order to accommodate that expectation, he priced his product higher than the

16

amount he expected to receive. Unfortunately, Stephanie was not approaching the transaction with the negotiation culture in mind. She expected the artist to ask for the value of the painting. She didn't anticipate a "cushion" built in to the asking price. If she had, she'd have received a better deal.

How does this situation apply to real life? In some situations, service providers who cater to engaged couples assume that negotiation is going to occur. They may anticipate this negotiation by adopting a higher pricing structure. This is in no way to portray these service providers as dishonest or profit-hungry. It's simply a cultural difference. For example, by pricing his services a little higher, a photographer can offer bonuses like additional photographs, added time photographing the wedding, or even special packages and deals on the photography service. He expects to negotiate with the couple-to-be, and because of that expectation, his initial quote has some "wiggle room."

It can be difficult to determine whether or not you're dealing with someone accustomed to a culture of negotiation. What if you offer to pay a lower price and send the photographer, or other service provider, into an offended rage? (Note: this is highly unlikely to happen, but it is a common irrational concern). This is what causes so many people to simply avoid negotiating altogether. In a later chapter, we'll discuss how to dispel these fears and treat negotiation like a commonplace conversation.

Communicating openly and honestly with the vendors and service providers on your wedding planning list is the best way to get the best value during the planning process. Admittedly, negotiation is unfamiliar territory for most. If you feel like you're out of your depth in the world of negotiation, you're not alone. Unlike Crump and Grump, we use money with a set value, which reduces the necessity of conversation. Currency has created a seller's world: one where the seller sets the price and the buyer pays without questioning.

Hopefully, though, you see why negotiation is an important step when purchasing services rather than products. You need to understand precisely what you're paying for, and photographers, caterers, wedding coordinators, etc. should be prepared to tell you precisely why their services cost what they do. Additionally, it's important to avoid falling into the Negotiation Culture Trap. Stephanie's artist wasn't trying to cheat her, but he expected negotiation that never occurred, and Stephanie ended up paying more.

The world has changed throughout the years, and our "negotiation consciousness" has faded, but it's important to realize that you can get it back. Marsha Lichtenstein puts it beautifully when she says, "It's not that you can't negotiate. It's that you haven't been taught."
Your Starting Place

The first step in overcoming any problem is, of course, to admit that there is a problem. In this chapter, we've acknowledged that our society has a general aversion to the dance of negotiation. There are many reasons for this. Some of this aversion can be explained simply by the changes of history. As we moved away from trading goods for goods or services for services and embraced a culture of currency, the need for negotiation started to dissipate. Some of it can be explained culturally: there are still some businesses or services where haggling and bartering is expected, creating a negotiation culture.

Still, most of our aversion to negotiation can only be explained personally. The plain truth is we often hate to negotiate. This is a hatred that must be overcome, especially for couples planning a wedding. Below, you'll find some of the most common reasons given by engaged couples to explain their aversion to negotiation. If any of these statements resonate with you, personally, pay careful attention to that statement. This is the belief that you will have to overcome to embrace successful negotiation techniques. Unless you put your distaste for negotiation to rest, you will find it very difficult to use negotiation tactics while planning your wedding.

Which of these statements apply to you?

- **I've never negotiated for anything before, and I have no idea how to begin.** If this is you, don't worry! By the end of this book you will have a thorough understanding of basic negotiation techniques.
- **I'm afraid that if I try to negotiate for basic wedding services I will make the service provider angry or annoyed.** This is a common reason for negotiation fear, and we'll discuss overcoming this type of fear in a later chapter.
- **I don't know what I should expect to pay for wedding services.** Arming yourself with this kind of knowledge is a crucial step of negotiation, and we'll discuss it in-depth later on.
- **I don't think negotiation is appropriate in today's modern society.** As discussed, this is a common misconception. Negotiation is not only appropriate, it's often necessary to determine the value of a service.
- **I've had a bad experience negotiating before, and I'm not willing to go through that again.** This is quite common. Many negotiating newbies make a critical error in an early negotiation experience. Remember, though, that negotiation is a dance. Practice makes perfect, and a bad first experience doesn't mean that all future encounters will be negative.
- **Negotiation will just add stress to my life. I'd rather pay what they ask with no questions.** This is a deadly misconception! Failing to negotiate can actually result in more stress than good negotiation. Don't think of negotiation as an argument; think of it as a healthy discussion. We'll

discuss positive, stress-free, collaborative negotiation in a later chapter.

- **I'm doing this without my fiancé, and I don't think I have what it takes.** Women are often left in charge of the wedding planning process, and many women struggle with presenting a position of power in a negotiation. In fact, Linda Babcock and Sara Laschever, authors of Ask For It, completed months of research that reveals men are four times as likely to initiate a negotiation as women. This is a common issue that can be overcome, and we'll discuss great tips for women in a future chapter.

Chapter 2
NEGOTIATIONS are NON-NEGOTIABLE

If you're still struggling to understand why negotiations are such an important part of the wedding planning process (of if you're trying to convince a feet-dragging fiancé of the importance of tackling this issue together) then this chapter is for you. Believe it or not, the way you handle negotiations while planning your wedding can prep you for successfully navigating the choppy waters of marriage. So, if you want to "groom your groom" or you personally want to cultivate a positive and productive self-image, working together to negotiate wedding contracts is invaluable.

Marriage is the Biggest Negotiation of Your Life

For couples with an insurmountable aversion to negotiations, married life is bound to be a whopping surprise. At its very foundation, a marriage is an agreement between two people. Two individuals spend time together and decide they like one another. Affinity turns into affection, which in turn transforms into blissful love. And while it's not the purpose of this book to dump heaping pails of reality on you and your intended, you probably already know that bliss isn't a guaranteed state of mind in a marriage. There will come days of strife, pain, and struggle. That's where negotiation comes into play.

It's understandable that couples don't want to view their marriage as a negotiated contract. It sounds cold and unromantic. This, however, reflects a skewed vision of negotiating. Stop thinking of negotiations as a slick-haired car salesman trying to trick you into buying a lemon. Start, instead, to think of negotiating as a mutual and honest exchange of values. We'll go into greater detail about a positive negotiation mentality in a later chapter, but for now understand this simple truth: negotiation is the only way to make a marriage work. It's a form of mediation. It's a machine that inputs two separate sets of desires and outputs one compromise that pleases both parties. Effective negotiation will be the core of a successful marriage.

What better place to start practicing than during the wedding planning phase? Couples who negotiate together before they are married will learn valuable skills. Here are situations where you and your intended will benefit when you start by learning effective negotiation:

- Conflict Resolution: Married couples get into arguments; it's inevitable. Good negotiation skills will help each person express their opinion in a healthy and effective way. Resolving conflict can help you grow closer as a couple.
- Goal Reaching: Negotiation skills are closely tied to goal reaching skills. By envisioning the end result together, couples can determine the steps necessary to reach even the most lofty goals.
- Financial Planning: Budget struggles are the number one cause of failed marriages. Good negotiation can help couples save money on big purchases and understand the value of healthy budgeting and financial planning.

22

- Child Rearing: Any parent will tell you that raising a child is nothing but negotiations from sunup to sundown. Parents must negotiate with each other, and they also have to communicate clearly and patiently with their children. Believe it or not, learning to negotiate during the wedding planning process can actually help couples develop valuable child-rearing skills.
- Purchasing a Home: The biggest purchase that the majority of married couples will make is the purchase of a new home. This process is peppered with negotiations from start to finish. By learning skills like clear communication, the ability to walk away from a bad deal, and other negotiation tactics, couples can approach this daunting task with confidence.
- Purchasing an Automobile: Getting the best deal on a new minivan is easier when couples have worked together to develop effective negotiation skills.
- Working with Employees or Customers: Negotiation is critical in the workplace; it will help you handle conflict with employees, co-workers, and customers. It can also help with career ascension by teaching values like self-worth and self-promotion. This is especially crucial for women who are far less likely to ask for a raise or pursue career advancement than men.
- Saying No: This simple skill may not sound like much, but it can make the difference between a life that is overflowing with commitments and a life that is well-paced and manageable. Practicing negotiation can help you learn when and how to say "no" to friends, family members, work associates, strangers, children, and even your spouse.

Planning a wedding is a great early experience in which to practice the art of negotiation. As revealed in this chapter, learning these basic skills will be invaluable throughout your life, and you'll be able to step lightly and easily through future negotiations, securing the services or goods you need at a price you can afford.

The Business of Negotiation

There's one more important benefit to be gained through wedding negotiations: preparation for the business world. While this book focuses predominantly on negotiations from a wedding planning perspective, negotiation plays an enormous role in the business community. Linda Babcock and Sara Laschever are the authors of Ask For It and the creators of WomenDontAsk.com. I encourage you to explore their book, as it is one of the leading resources for women in the business community, but I briefly want to mention some of their research here.

Did you know that women earn roughly 77 cents for every dollar earned by a man in the business world? This statistic is shocking because of the cause for this income difference. Women aren't earning less because they are less qualified, less experienced, or less professional. Studies show that they are earning less because they aren't asking for more. Men, on the other hand, approach negotiation with gusto.

In Ask For It, Babcock and Laschever reveal that a mere $5,000 increase in the starting salary of a low-paying position can grow into an extra $750,000 dollars over forty years. Women who don't negotiate may be missing out on nearly a million dollars in extra retirement income: all because of one missed negotiation.

Planning a wedding is often one of the first major milestones in a young woman's life. With little to no experience negotiating, budgeting, and planning, this event represents a fertile training ground for a woman's future. Don't shy away from negotiation potential.

You might just be practicing the priceless skills that will transform your future.

Chapter 3
UP for DISCUSSION

One of the biggest hurdles that engaged couples face while planning a wedding is indecision regarding which wedding services merit negotiation tactics and which are better left un-negotiated. Remember the Starbucks latte that we discussed last chapter? Negotiating the cost of a latte isn't going to be a valuable time investment because the most you are going to be able to save is a few pennies (if you aren't laughed out of the store by the barista).

Time is money, and negotiation should be saved for instances where real value can be secured. This chapter discusses some of the basic expenses associated with wedding planning. It provides helpful information about the "wiggle room" for negotiation associated with each of these services.

Let's take a look:

Wedding Services with Room for Negotiation

- **Wedding Photography and Videography:** One of the first services that couples consider when planning a wedding is often photography and videography. It also happens to be one of the more expensive services. Thankfully, there is plenty of room for negotiation with photographers and videographers. Couples can ask questions about special packages, seasonal deals and savings, negotiate reduced prices for multiple photographers, large photos and canvas prints, photo booths, and much more.
- **Wedding Coordinator or Wedding Planner:** Hiring a wedding planner or a wedding coordinator will dramatically reduce the stress you experience on your wedding day, but it's important to communicate fully and openly through negotiation to be sure you're getting the precise services you need. There is plenty of room for negotiation with these service providers, as most of them customize their services fully to accommodate a client's needs.
- **Ceremony Facilities:** If you need facilities for your wedding, like a church, meeting hall, event center, country club, etc., you'll want to spend some time negotiating before you sign the contract. Negotiating the contract for a facility rental will ensure you know all of your options. Can catering be added at a reduced rate? What if you provide your own tables, chairs, decorations, dishes, utensils, etc.? If you pay cash in advance for the rental, can you negotiate a lower price? These are all valuable questions to ask.
- **Catering and Table Service:** Caterers and wait staff can help to elevate your event, but the total price for these services can quickly add up. Negotiation is an important step in securing a catering or table service contract. For this wedding service, though, negotiation is less about price and more about getting exactly the type of food and service you want. Working closely with a caterer will help

couples avoid unexpected surprises and disappointment on the day of the wedding.

- **Gift Registries:** Did you know that you can negotiate special pricing and savings when registering for gifts? Big brand stores like Bed, Bath, and Beyond and Target may offer coupons and discounts on certain products when couples register for gifts. Additionally, if you register for items at a smaller, boutique-style store, there is even more room for negotiation. Understand that a smaller store will receive a big boon when hundreds of guests start purchasing items for a wedding. They may be quite willing to lower prices, passing on savings to your guests.
- **Wedding Music:** Disc jockeys and wedding bands are prime real estate for successful negotiations. Because the cost of this service will vary widely based on location, length of performance time, travel requirements, and other variables, negotiating an affordable contract that pleases both parties is critical.
- **Wedding Attire Purchase and Rentals:** Every wedding party needs dresses, tuxedos, suits, and other purchased or rented items, and negotiating contracts for these items is a great way to save money. For example, many tuxedo rental companies will provide the groom's tuxedo for free if the groomsmen rent their tuxes from the same location. Be sure to ask questions about savings and package deals when negotiating these types of contracts.
- **Transportation and Destination Weddings:** Planning on taking a trip with family and friends to celebrate your nuptials? Don't just ask everyone to purchase airfare or travel accommodations individually. Negotiating event contracts with travel agents, hotels, destination wedding resorts, and airline companies will save you hundreds of dollars.
- **Wedding Packages:** Some locations specialize in full-scale wedding events, and they may be able to offer incredible savings to engaged couples. By packaging together services like photography, catering, event location rental, music, and lodging, the overall cost of the service can be reduced.

While planning a wedding at one of these locations can reduce stress, the importance of expert negotiation increases because of all the options available.

Is Anything Off-Limits?

One thing that many engaged couples wonder when planning a wedding is whether any part of the ceremony is "off-limits" as far as negotiation is concerned. Nobody wants to risk offending a high quality service provider, and negotiating prices can sometimes feel like short-changing a talented individual. In very general terms, there is nothing that is officially off-limits for negotiation. As we'll discuss in a later chapter, it never hurts to ask.

That said, some couples do feel that it is inappropriate to ask for a price reduction where a non-profit organization, like a church or other religious institution, is concerned. Renting a church facility or paying for the services of a clergyman, reverend, pastor, preacher, rabbi, etc. is often viewed as a donation, of sorts, to that organization's work. In these cases, it may be appropriate to simply pay the requested amount without excessive negotiation. Of course, couples should use their own intuition when deciding how much and when to negotiate. It's highly unlikely that anyone will be offended by a question about price.

Chapter 4
WOMEN and NEGOTIATION

When discussing negotiation, it's important to spend a little time acknowledging the different challenges that women face when entering the complex world of contract negotiation. For many women, negotiating is a completely new and foreign experience. Women face challenges like sexism, expectations that differ from those assigned to men, and different life experiences. All of these can work together to make negotiation especially tough on a woman.

The good news is it doesn't have to be this way. There is absolutely no reason why a woman cannot initiate a negotiation that is absolutely as productive, as healthy, and as empowering as that initiated by a man. Yes, women may have to overcome preconceived notions and gender-specific obstacles, but numerous studies have shown that women can be quite capable negotiators. Let's take a look at the negotiation world from a woman's perspective.

Women and Wedding Planning

First, let's clear the air by addressing something that thousands of women have shaken their fists at through the ages: wedding planning often falls on the shoulders of the female. From a man's perspective, his work ends once the diamond ring slides onto the lady's ring finger. From that moment on, it's the bride-to-be who is expected to turn a single answered question into a full-scale event that will initiate a life of marriage.

Why in the world is this the case? Sorry, ladies, the answer isn't going to make you feel better. On the one hand, wedding planning often falls to the woman simply because women are statistically more likely to have strong opinions about the ceremony itself. This is a generalization, yes, but it is a generalization because it is often true. Men don't often have strong opinions about the types of flowers adorning the aisles of the chapel. They don't really care on what paper the invitations are printed. They're too often hopeless when it comes to choosing bridesmaid dress colors, selecting a menu, or dreaming up the most beautiful cake to ever be shoved into an unsuspecting bride's mouth.

Is this always true? Well, of course not. There are many women who have been delighted by a groom who is attentive, vocal about his opinions, supportive, and engaging. There are many other women who are awarded a noncommittal shrug in response to every wedding-related question. Whatever your particular situation, it's important to be willing to shoulder the responsibility of negotiating wedding contracts. If you're pleasantly surprised by a helpful groom-to-be, that's wonderful. On the other hand, if you find yourself in a classic "Whatever you want, honey" situation, you'll be ready.

Why is Negotiation Tougher for Women?

Since the responsibility often falls on the woman's shoulders, it would seem logical that the world would be prepared to adequately deal with women when it comes to negotiation. Unfortunately, that's often not the case. Negotiation is almost always tougher for women than it is for men. This is easily identified in the differences between how men and women view negotiation. Marsha Lichtenstein, a guide and coach for women who want to learn to negotiate, once revealed in a presentation that men and women had very different responses when asked, during a study, to describe an analogy for negotiation.

According to the study, performed by Linda Babcock and Sara Laschever, men most often said that negotiation is like "winning a ballgame." This is an incredible positive image. Not only do men equate negotiation with a sport that offers excitement, challenges, and fun, but they also equate the general idea of negotiation with a positive end result. They didn't compare it to playing a ballgame, but winning one. When a man is asked to describe negotiation, he already visualizes himself winning the game.

What did Lichtenstein discover when she asked women the same question? Perhaps unsurprisingly, women equated negotiation with going to the dentist. Notice the contrast. Women view negotiation, not as a fun activity, but with an experience that requires them to be sitting submissively in a chair, vulnerable, exposed, and often in pain.

Why do women view the dance of negotiation in such a negative light? Marsha Lichtenstein has an answer for that, too. Her years of research and experience have revealed that women are often presented with conflicting expectations. In the workplace, employees are expected to promote themselves, reach for the sky, break the glass ceiling, etc. Employers expect their employees to rise within the business. At the same time, women are expected to be demure, kind, polite, submissive, and even quiet. How can a woman be both of these things?

A man who is headstrong and determined is glorified and lauded as a perfect example of heroism. He's pursuing the American Dream. He's confident and capable. A woman with the exact same characteristics is rarely viewed in the same positive light. She is seen as shrew-like, cold, calculating, belligerent, and abrasive. It's an unfair situation, but it's one that almost all women will have to face. Women are expected, according to Lichtenstein, to follow the rules. They're expected to refrain from being pushy or questioning authority. These expectations don't set women up to be the best negotiators.

The Dangers of Conflict Aversion

Because of this double-standard, women are often groomed to adopt a life of conflict aversion. This is especially true in the workplace, where women accept longer hours and more difficult tasks than men while receiving less pay. Women sidestep conflict rather than addressing it head on. When it comes to planning your wedding (or negotiating anything in your life, for that matter), conflict aversion is almost always going to result in a win/lose situation. And you'll likely be on the losing end.

Conflict aversion may seem like a stress-free way to live. You can avoid confrontation, skip arguments that result in hurt feelings, be perceived as a pleasant and carefree individual, and coast through life without worry. In reality, conflict aversion is dangerous. Here are just a few of the ill effects of habitually avoiding conflict:

- Missed opportunities
- Low self-esteem
- Inability to communicate effectively
- Consistently being taken advantage of by others, either intentionally or unintentionally

- Excessive debt caused by the inability to say "no"
- Feelings of pent-up anger or resentment
- Irrational behavior and risk taking in order to escape or assert oneself
- Increased likelihood of substance abuse and other destructive behaviors

You can put this information to use right here and right now while you are planning your wedding. Recognize your tendency, if it exists, to avoid conflict and accept the hand you're dealt. Find within yourself a willingness to stand up for yourself, to create a positive self-image, and to communicate confidently and authoritatively. This doesn't mean you need to walk around looking for a fight. If the cashier accidentally charges you extra, for example, don't fly into a rage in order to combat gender expectations. However, you should be wary of the double standards placed on women, especially in regard to negotiation.

Negotiating, Not Emotiating

One of the untruths ingrained into the minds of women from early on is the fact that a strong tie to her emotions is the Achilles Heel of the woman. Women are perceived as weak simply because they are emotional. Emotion has no place in a successful negotiation, right? In order to walk out on top, one must be a shark: cold, alert, and predatorial. This is codswallop, and women need to stop swallowing it because it is robbing them of their most effective negotiation tactic!

SimpliLearn is an online course subgroup of the Project Management Institute, Incorporated. In one of their courses on conflict negotiation and resolution, they illustrate the significance of emotional intelligence. According to their research findings, the ability to empathize and emotionally connect with another party is a crucial step in successful conflict resolution. This flies in the face of conventional negotiation theory. Negotiators are often viewed as belligerent, fist-pounding men who storm out of the room in a huff when things aren't going their way.

We see this all the time in movies, television, and books. We view negotiation like an animal territorial ritual. When competing for a mate, male peacocks spread their beautiful tail feathers and strut around one another, trying to determine whose plumage is the plumpest. Male Bighorn Sheep run down steep mountainsides before bashing their horns into one another. This behavior is seen throughout the Animal Kingdom, and somewhere along the way we started assuming that this form of negotiation is the one that works the best.

According to SimpliLearn, however, the aspects often attributed to a woman (empathy, understanding, patience, composure, etc.) are the ones most likely to result in effective negotiation. The key, then, is to direct emotion rather than be controlled by it. Flying off the handle or breaking down in tears are, obviously, emotional responses that can derail a negotiation. Listening patiently, asking relevant questions, showing understanding and empathy, and speaking calmly are also emotional responses, but these emotional responses can turn a conflict into a win/win situation.

The Expert Negotiator Misconception

There's another problem that affects women: the expert negotiator misconception. Imagine, for a minute, a person who looks and acts like the best negotiator in the world. What does this person look like in your imagination? Most likely, it's a "he," and most likely he's slick, sneaky, and slimy. There was a children's show in the 1990s called Shining Time Station. One of the characters in this show was a man named Schemer. With his pinstripe suit and slicked back hair, Schemer was the epitome of successful negotiation. He was a penny-pinching, profit-thirsty individual who could probably have negotiated himself out of an alligator's jaws if given the time.

That may be the initial image we conjure in our minds of a successful negotiator, but that image couldn't be further from the truth. Successful negotiators are actually empathetic, emotional, patient, and understanding individuals. Negotiators who walk away on the winning side of a negotiation are, quite surprisingly, the ones who don't view the process as a win/lose situation to begin with. We'll discuss in detail the benefits of collaborative negotiation mindsets in a future chapter, but it's important at this stage to realize that women don't have to be at a disadvantage when it comes to negotiation.

The world may expect men to be the best in the biz when it comes to haggling. The world may think women who negotiate are pushy and obstinate. The world is wrong.

The same qualities that the world equates with "feminine grace" are some of the same qualities that create superb negotiators.

Chapter 5
DEVELOP a HEALTHY NEGOTIATION MINDSET

G et ready, because this chapter is going to reveal the first and foremost key to initiating and completing a successful negotiation. Are you ready for the big reveal? Here it is:

Successful negotiation depends, almost entirely, on your own mind.

Did you get that? Many people mistakenly believe that negotiation depends fully on the other party's willingness to compromise. While it's true that you're not going to get very far with a purposefully belligerent individual, you have an incredible amount of power to change the course of a negotiation, change someone's mind, and change the attitude of the entire conversation. All that is required is for you to change the way you think.

One of the tenets of the SimpliLearn course on successful negotiation is the basic definition of negotiation. SimpliLearn's experts wisely state that "Negotiation means discussion intended to produce agreement." For some reason, we trump up negotiation in our minds and turn it into something scary, intense, or downright evil.

Remember that imagination exercise we did in the last chapter regarding the image of an expert negotiator. Let's take that a little further. Take a moment to imagine a scene from a movie; let's say it's a movie about a high stakes deal on Wall Street. The two parties, buyer and seller, are meeting at the top of a New York City skyrise. Attorneys and accountants are gathered in a smoke-filled room around a long, mahogany table. Can you picture it?

Now, negotiations are underway. What does the atmosphere of the room look like in your mind? If you're like most people, you're probably picturing a lot of whispering, conspiratorial behavior, cold stares, masculine and aggressive posturing, and maybe a bit of shouting thrown in as a bonus. That's a fairly common image that most people conjure up in their minds when envisioning negotiation.

Surprise: that's actually the recipe for the worst ever negotiation. Odds are good that both parties will walk out of an atmosphere like that upset, angry, and frustrated. Negotiation that results in a win/win situation isn't a shouting match. It's not even a competition. It's a dialogue. It is communication and discussion intended to produce compromise.

Remember the popular film Pretty Woman, starring Richard Gere and Julia Roberts? In the film, Gere plays the cliché we just discussed: a stereotypically cut-throat negotiator. In his attempts to make the deal of his lifetime by purchasing a family-owned company, though, he realizes that his strategy is not working. There's a critical scene in the film where Gere dismisses his expert team of negotiators, looks directly into the eyes of the aging business owner, and starts having a conversation rather than making a sales pitch. When you watch the film, you can see the body language of the business owner change dramatically. He relaxes. He begins to listen to what Gere is saying. He asks questions. He grows more comfortable. He develops a tone of trust and honesty. This is a successful negotiation, and the audience immediately knows that a solution is within reach.

If you simply make a few changes to your state of mind before engaging in negotiations, you'll dramatically improve your chances for success. Let's look at four big mindset changes that need to occur.

Fear Has No Place at the Table

First, there is no room whatsoever for fear at a negotiation table. The trouble with fear is twofold. First, it's completely unnecessary. Second, it leads to negotiation mistakes that can derail an otherwise successful conversation.

The vast majority of first-time negotiators have an irrational fear of negotiation. They tremble at the prospect of voicing an opinion, expressing a concern, or asking for something extra. Where in the world does this fear come from? The answer is probably that figment of imagination created at the beginning of this chapter. We create visions of being yelled at, of the other party storming from the room, at losing out on the chance of a lifetime.

The truth is, these things are not going to happen. Instead of approaching negotiation from a mindset of fear, approach the discussion with a mindset of "What do I have to lose?" For example, if you can't afford to pay the price a photographer is asking for the services you require, communicate that to the photographer. One of three scenarios may occur.

First, the photographer may say that he or she cannot adjust the price at all. If that's the case, you can look elsewhere. You've lost nothing because you couldn't afford to pay full price in the first place. You've actually escaped the chance of being talked into a service that exceeded your budget. The second option is a compromise. Perhaps the photographer can eliminate some of the services or reveal a money-saving option for you to consider. This promotes a conversation where both of you can agree. Third, the photographer may say she understands your budget restrictions and she's willing to give you a discount.

What have you got to lose by negotiating? Absolutely nothing. What have you to gain by initiating a discussion and seeking an agreement? Everything.

The second problem with fear is it leads to irrational responses and emotional outbursts. Fear may lead to anger as a coping mechanism. A fearful individual in a negotiation will project his fears onto the other party. Even if, say, a wedding coordinator is explaining pricing levels and services very rationally, your fear could cause you to misinterpret what is being said. You risk offending or ostracizing the other party.

According to Dr. Irena O'Brien, a research scientist who specializes in neuroscience and personal achievement, fear is also one of the largest contributors to procrastination. Your irrational fear of negotiating with a caterer, for example, could lead to you putting the task off day after day. This adds to your overall stress levels, and it can also force you to compromise on something because you'll have to scramble to secure a caterer at the last minute. Procrastination is an unnecessary response to an unnecessary emotion.

Fear is better left off the table to begin with.

Embracing Self-Worth

So how can you counteract fear? How can you approach negotiations with a bold and confident air? The trick is to embrace your own sense of self-worth. We discussed some of the messages that Marsha Lichtenstein found women receive on a daily basis, especially in the workplace. Women are expected to follow orders, respect authority, and go with the crowd. This is a serious issue, according to Lichtenstein, because these messages start to turn into ingrained beliefs. She says the three most dangerous beliefs are:

- I don't deserve it.
- I'm a fraud.
- What's being offered is good enough for me.

These three beliefs will destroy your negotiation potential if they are not addressed. If you enter a negotiation doubting whether or not you deserve what you want, you'll accept whatever is offered without question. If you doubt your own sincerity, adopting an "I'm a fraud" attitude, you'll be easily convinced to accept something you don't want. Finally, if you convince yourself that whatever is offered is "good enough," you'll end negotiations before you've achieved your desires.

Changing these beliefs starts with intense self-reflection and self-promotion. Make a list of your good qualities. Write out what you want in your wedding ceremony and why it's important to you. Evaluate your desires and convince yourself that your desires are valid and valuable. Before you go into a negotiation, say these three statements to yourself.

- I know what I want.
- I know why I want it.
- I know where I can compromise and where I need to hold my ground.

If you can say these three statements with absolute honesty, you'll be ready to face a negotiation. If you act confident, you'll start to feel confident.

Conversation vs. Conflict

Earl Nightingale was an amazing motivational speaker and published author who rose to prominence in the 1950s. He hosted a personal development radio show on WGN, and his consistently helpful advice led him to be known as the "Dean of Personal Development." Marsha Lichtenstein features a brilliant Earl Nightingale quote on her blog at WomenNegotiate. com:

> "Attitudes truly are contagious...so ask yourself one question: Is mine worth catching?"

Don't you just love that imagery? We think of contagion as a sniffly outbreak waiting to wreak havoc on us at the airport. But what if we started viewing our attitudes as contagious states of mind? If you could change someone's attitude simply by being pleasant, understanding, and patient wouldn't you work extra hard to cultivate these character traits?

Nightingale was absolutely right: attitude is contagious, and this plays an extraordinarily significant role in negotiations. It's important to view a negotiation as a conversation rather than a conflict. Yes, there is conflict of a sort involved in just about every negotiation. The seller of a product or service wants to get the highest price possible. It's how he or she makes a living. The buyer, on the other hand, wants the best possible service or product at the lowest possible price. It's a situation that seems to put two people at odds with one another, but it doesn't have to be viewed that way.

One of the foundation layers of SimpliLearn's agile negotiation strategy is "inventing options for mutual gain." Instead of digging in your heels, crossing your arms, and insisting on your way, it may be helpful to create options that will benefit both parties. Try to find a compromise. Approach negotiation as an exchange of ideas rather than a fighting match to the death.

Of course, to accomplish this, you'll need to let go of that death grip you have on control.

Loosening Your Death Grip on Control

Have you ever heard someone called a "control freak"? You probably know exactly what that looks like. "Control freak" is a less-than-flattering term for someone who needs to be involved in every decision-making process, needs to have a hand in every project, and needs to see her every whim materialize. When a control freak starts to lose control, what does she do?

Well naturally, she freaks.

We all have a little bit of control freak deep down inside us, and the truth is that's not always a bad thing. An affinity for control can help us to improve our self-image, speak up and express our needs and desires, and avoid becoming a doormat in our myriad relationships.

When control becomes freaky, though, there's a problem. To negotiate successfully, you must find within yourself a willingness to relinquish some of the control in a situation. For negotiation to be a mutually-serving conversation rather than a conflict, both parties need to have equal control. Here are some ways you can let go of your need to control a situation:

- Make three lists when preparing for a negotiation. One list will include "must-haves," one should include "would-likes," and another can list "don't-cares." The items on your don't care list can be relinquished entirely to the other party. If you're meeting with a baker, maybe you don't really care how many tiers are on your wedding cake; you just want to ensure there is enough for everyone. Give the control of that situation over to the caterer. On the other hand, you may be very adamant that the icing is butter-cream rather than fondant. Express that to the baking professional.

- Take a breath. Reacting off the cuff after you hear disappointing news won't give you time to relinquish control and respond patiently and evenly. A desire for control can make us lash out, but taking a moment to collect yourself will help you put things in perspective.

- Keep a wedding planning journal. It's easy to lose sight of the true meaning of the wedding ceremony as you immerse yourself in the intricacies of planning. What's really important here? Is the color of the calla lilies in your bouquet going to dictate the success of the event? Or, do you simply want a lovely, family- and friend-filled day dedicated to celebrating the love between you and your partner? Keeping a journal and taking a step back from the negotiation processes will help you relinquish control.

- Practice, Practice, Practice. Here's a tip for the chronic control freak. If you have trouble relinquishing control over a situation, force yourself to give up some small measure of control during each negotiation even if it is unnecessary. When you meet with the band, tell them you don't care what they wear. When you coordinate with the photographer, let them decide whether to take pictures before or after the ceremony. Every time you compromise, you'll get a little better at it.

Successful negotiation is all about your initial mindset. It requires a mindset that must be carefully practiced and cultivated over time. Abandon your fears, recognize your own self-worth, initiate productive conversations, and don't get white-knuckled in your attempt to hold onto control. You will see your negotiations improve rapidly.

Chapter 6
NEGOTIATION PREP

Imagine that two couples are preparing to go on a once-in-a-lifetime, round-the-world road trip. Bob and Barbara have always wanted to see Europe. They make a modest income between the two of them, and they've saved up a month of vacation days to use up on their journey. Carl and Cassie also want to see the history and countryside of Europe. They've got the exact same budget and number of available vacation days as Bob and Barbara. These two couples want to see the same sights, experience the same adventure, and get the most out of their holiday.

However, the couples are about to embark on their journeys in completely different ways. Bob and Barbara decide that a spur-of-the-moment trip is romantic, exciting, and adventurous. They don't want to get bogged down in the stresses of planning, researching, and budgeting. So, they catch a cab to the airport and hop on the first available flight to Europe. Once there, they book a room at the first hotel they come to. Their trip is a whirlwind; they take trains, boats, cabs, and rental cars from city to city, with no advanced plans made.

Carl and Cassie are another story. They take several weeks to plan their trip. Cassie researches travel arrangements by comparing the cost of train passes, airfare, vehicle rental charges, and cab fares. She also looks up hotels, motels, and hostels, comparing prices and reviewing customer ratings to find the best deals. Carl spends his time plotting out the most time-efficient way to travel from country to country. He creates a vacation itinerary, complete with the times and dates major tourist attractions, like Buckingham Palace, are open for tours. Only after the trip is completely planned do Carl and Cassie set out on their adventure.

Who has the better trip? Well, Bob and Barb ran out of money by the time they reached Barcelona. They still had a week of vacation days left, but no money with which to enjoy them. They also missed out on the Louvre in Paris and the Coliseum in Rome because they weren't open when the two lovebirds visited those cities. Their hotel rooms leaked when it rained. They were stranded in Ireland for a week straight because all outbound traffic was booked solid. Yes, they made memories. Yes, they enjoyed a lovely experience that helped them grow as a couple.

But they didn't have the trip that Carl and Cassie had. Carl and Cassie knew what to expect before they ever arrived in Europe. There were a couple of hiccups on the journey, but Carl had researched alternative tourist attractions and Cassie had contingency travel and lodging plans booked in advance. At the end of their vacation, these two had money to spare, and they used it to add a traditional English Rose garden to their backyard, bringing a little bit of Europe back home.

Clearly, this little cautionary tale has a point. Both couples went to Europe. Both couples enjoyed their vacation time.

Both couples will have lifelong memories to enjoy. However, Carl and Cassie got more out of the journey, spent less, and experienced less stress and disappointment than Bob and Barbara.

What made the difference? Preparation. Planning a wedding is like planning a road trip. Yes, you can jump in head first, schedule wedding services with no plan of action, accept the first contracts offered to you by service providers, and still end up with a beautiful wedding.

With a little preparation, though, you can enter into negotiations to reduce the cost of wedding services, ensure you get the services you want and need, and cut your overall stress level in half. All you have to do is research, budget, prepare, and plan.

This chapter represents an essential part of the negotiation process, and everything covered in this chapter should happen before negotiations ever begin. Preparation is half the battle with negotiation. Equip yourself with information, details, and advanced planning, and you'll be well on your way to successfully completing your first negotiation.

Research, Research, Research

Remember those high school and college days where you spent hours marching through the Internet jungles looking for resources to complete that endless term paper? If you're like most people, you probably thought those days were long behind you, but expert negotiation requires expert research. Unless you are well-informed about the business with which you are meeting, the services offered, comparative prices and services offered by other businesses, and the latest trends in the wedding service industry, you'll have no starting ground for your negotiations.

What kind of cakes are people getting to serve 100 guests? How much do these cakes cost, on average? What's the average cost of a wedding DJ? How many hours do you need the DJ to perform? What if you want a full-sized orchestra? How many photographs do you want taken? Do you want an engagement photo session?

All of these questions can be answered by researching the wedding service industry. Today, millions of pages of facts, price lists, and other information are available at your finger-tips. Linda Babcock and Sara Laschever, founders of Women-DontAsk.com and negotiation coaches for women, advocate using the internet for research to collect facts. These facts become tools when used in a negotiation setting. In their popular book, Ask For It, they explain the necessity of this research:

> "Setting the right target… a target that's high but fair, ambitious but appropriate, well founded but also realistic, requires research… If you want to negotiate the price of a product or service… you need to know the best rates and prices available--where to find the best discounts, who's offering combination packages or buyer's incentives, whether you'll be sacrificing quality if you push for a lower price (and where that threshold lies), and how to find the most reliable vendors, providers, or partners" (Babcock, Laschever *Women Don't Ask* 91).

You can use the pages included at the back of this book to keep track of your research for each service you require. Focus on deciding exactly what you want at your wedding, anticipating costs, and brainstorming questions to ask during the negotiation process.

Establish a Bottom Line and an Exit Strategy

One of the reasons why engaged couples fear negotiations

is the misconception that they are slippery traps intended to snare unsuspecting consumers. Nobody wants to sign a contract for a service that is too expensive, too extravagant, or otherwise unsuitable, and yet that's often what happens because couples are unprepared for the "hard sell" tactics of the wedding service provider.

Negotiations don't have to be head-to-head conflicts. They can be treated like collaborative conversations. Still, it's important to remember that the seller and the buyer have different goals they hope to achieve during the negotiation. A seller wants to advertise his or her services. A seller wants to offer extras and add-ons to increase the final contract cost. A seller wants to position himself in the best possible light, and convince the buyer that he's offering exactly what she needs.

Sometimes, the seller and the buyer are in perfect agreement. Sometimes they aren't. If you prepare for a negotiation by establishing a bottom line and practicing some efficient exit strategies, you'll have very little risk of sliding into a slippery contract that disappoints you.

First: the bottom line. Decide before you ever schedule a meeting with a wedding service provider how much you can afford to pay for the service. This represents an absolute maximum. No matter what happens, you must promise yourself that you will not exceed this budget max. Similarly, establish a bottom line regarding the bare minimum service you are willing to settle for. Maybe this is a number of photographs taken. Maybe this represents the length of a DJ's performance, the quality of wedding vehicles, the color and style of bridesmaids' dresses, etc. When you know your bottom line, you'll know if an exit strategy is necessary.

An exit strategy helps you walk away from a deal that isn't satisfying your bottom line requirements. Marsha Lichtenstein, of WomenNegotiate.com, released a report in 2013 addressing the problem of women being consistently unable to say "no." Women often feel guilty over a negative response, and this guilt pressures them into accepting situations that simply don't meet their requirements. Her advice: keep it short, and keep it simple.

Come up with a direct, confident, and to-the-point line that expresses your disinterest in the offered contract:

- No, I'm sorry. Thank you for your time.
- This isn't working for me.
- I'd like to consider other businesses, thank you.
- I think I have what I need. I'll be in touch.

Your "no" doesn't have to be involved and complex. You don't owe anyone an explanation for your decision. If you don't like the contract offered, and there are no options that work for you and the seller, offer a short "No, thank you," shake hands, and leave. It really can be that simple.

Decide Not to Decide

One final admonition for this chapter: it's important to remember that you don't have to begin and end negotiations in one fell swoop. It's ok to take some time to consider your options, meet with other service providers, examine your wedding budget, reevaluate your needs and desires, and take a big breath before signing on the dotted line. Before you schedule a meeting with a wedding service provider, decide not to decide. Tell yourself that you are going to discuss options with the service provider, but you are going to leave the negotiation open-ended while you consider your options.

Often, the "sellers" on the other end of the negotiation table want to get a deal agreed upon and signed in one sitting. This is a strategy employed by the other side because sellers know that the marketplace is highly competitive. Take auto sales-men, for example. They push so hard to encourage consumers to make a buying decision while on the lot because they know that once a consumer walks away, the chances of making a deal decrease considerably. Auto salesmen aren't trying to cheat or swindle consumers by pressuring them to make a de-cision. They are, however, concerned with getting the consum-er's business, and observation has taught them that consumers who walk away from the car lot are oftentimes consumers who never return.

It's your responsibility, as the buyer and the lead negotiator, to insist that you are offered time and space to consider the con-tract at hand. At the same time, you can alleviate the seller's concerns and anxiety by expressing, again, your interest in the product or service being offered. Here's a sample situation.

Sheila is planning her wedding, and the first stop on her list is the baker who she'd like to make her cake. The baker shows her all the options, the prices, and the variables. Sheila has asked all of her questions and provided information about her budget and her specific needs. The baker invites Sheila to make a decision and pulls out a standard contract. Instead of signing and paying the deposit, though, Sheila wants to take some time to discuss the cake with her fiancé, her parents, and her friends.

She doesn't just walk out and say, "I'll think about it," though. Sheila truly likes this baker. She's excited about the quality, taste, and appearance of the cakes this baker makes. To satisfy her own need for time without worrying the baker, she says:

"I love your work, and I'm seriously considering you as the baker for my wedding. Instead of rushing into a decision, I'd like to talk it over with some of my family and friends. Can we schedule a follow-up meeting to finalize the purchase?"

Sheila affirmed the baker by praising his work. She also expressed the seriousness of her intentions and further alleviated the baker's anxiety by scheduling a follow-up meeting. Now, the baker doesn't feel like he has to pressure her to make an immediate decision. In fact, when Sheila shows up next week to sign the papers, the baker offers her a 10% discount to guarantee her business: a win-win situation.

There is no substitute for advanced preparation when it comes to negotiation. Researching companies, competitors, wedding service trends, and comparable businesses will help you know exactly what you want. Establishing a bottom line will prevent you from spending excessively as you enter into negotiations. Exit strategies offer simple, effective ways to walk away from deals that are either too expensive or simply not what you want. And completing negotiations in stages will reduce stress and provide opportunities to fully consider the offered deal.

Chapter 7
The VANILLA ICE NEGOTIATION STRATEGY

The 1990s were a heyday for parachute pants, neon colors, synthesizers, boom boxes, and embarrassing rap songs. Fair warning: this chapter, though critical to the negotiation training process, may bring to the surface a few unfortunate 1990s memories. If you ever found yourself standing in front of the bathroom mirror attempting to impress your reflection as you recited the full rap to the classic Vanilla Ice song "Ice Ice Baby," well then this chapter will make you feel right at home.

As it turns out, those embarrassing attempts at rap were actually significant experiences preparing us for the negotiation of our lives. That iconic first line: "Stop, collaborate, and listen" can be used as a 3-step guide for completing a successful negotiation. If you need to stop reading this book while you crimp your hair, find your magenta scrunchie, and crank up the tunes of yesteryear, that's understandable.

The Vanilla Ice Negotiation Strategy will be here when you return.

Stop

It may sound odd to start a negotiation strategy with the word "Stop," but this step can prevent you from completely derailing a negotiation before it even begins. There is a tendency to approach negotiations like a battle. We discussed this conflict mindset in a previous chapter. Treating a negotiation like a conflict can cause people to overreact, speak out of turn, ignore opportunities for compromise or collaboration, etc.

Aggressive or argumentative behavior does more than simply offend or ostracize the other party. It puts you in a defensive position. Rather than leading the negotiation by expressing your needs and desires, asking questions, and steering the conversation toward an agreement, confrontational behavior will put the other party in control of the situation. You'll be far less likely to exit the negotiation with a contract that satisfies your needs.

Where does this defensive posturing come from? Why do so many first-time negotiators make the mistake of puffing up, getting angry, and arguing from the comparatively weak position of hostility rather than calmly and confidently expressing their needs? The answer is probably an innate sense of inferiority or an underlying fear that the bargainer doesn't truly deserve the best bargain. This is especially true of women. While there is a wide variety of perspectives amongst female empowerment coaches and business professionals, my colleagues and I definitely agree on one thing: there is no room for female self-deprecation at the negotiation table. Unless you've convinced yourself that you deserve the best deal possible in a negotiation, you are going to find it impossible to convince others. That creeping self-doubt will manifest itself as anger, frustration, impatience, or confrontation.

The first step of the Vanilla Ice Negotiation Strategy requires you to apply the brakes if you feel like you are falling into a defensive position. Stop yourself from speaking angrily, arguing rather than conversing, speaking without thinking, or speaking out of turn. Stop. Take a breath. Excuse yourself, if necessary. Tell yourself that pursuing the negotiation is worth it to you, and tell yourself that you are worth pursuing the negotiation. Then move on to the second step.

Collaborate

Roger Fisher and William Ury wrote a best-selling book in 1981 called Getting To Yes. The book focuses solely on tactics that both sides of a negotiation can use to eliminate stalling and heel-digging and reach a win/win type of agreement. One of Fisher's and Ury's main admonishments was a shift in focus. Negotiators often tended to use position-based bargaining tactics, rather than interest-based bargaining tactics, and this was derailing many big-business negotiations in the 80s.

In their book, Ask for It, Linda Babcock and Sara Laschever explain the difference between these two bargaining standpoints in greater detail:

> "In position-based bargaining, negotiators announce what they want or what they're determined to see happen and spend the rest of the negotiation defending that position. In interest-based bargaining, negotiators try to understand the interests--the needs, goals, constraints, and pressures--behind each position and then look for a variety of ways to satisfy those interests" (Babcock, Laschever *Women Don't Ask* 167).

We can use this important distinction in the second step of our Vanilla Ice Negotiation Strategy. In this step, it's important to foster a collaborative attitude during the negotiation. Collaboration is a conversation where both parties are allowed to express their interests. Here's a helpful example.

Karen wants to hire a wedding decorator. She wants an individual who is available starting two days before the wedding ceremony. She wants someone with experience, someone with resources, and someone who has evidenced responsibility and dedication in the past. These are all her positions, not her interests. If Karen were to unload these interests during a negotiation, she might find that the wedding decorator she most wants to hire is unavailable two days before the wedding. The wedding decorator can only begin work the day before the wedding, and so Karen and the wedding planner are at an impasse.

If Karen were to express her interests, rather than her position, though, the situation could be quite different. Karen's interests are finding a wedding decorator who will help alleviate some of the stress associated with the wedding. She wants the wedding decorator to start two days before because that is when flowers, table decorations, chairs, tents, and other necessities will arrive. When Karen expresses her interests, the wedding decorator offers to send an associate to the wedding site two days before the wedding to receive and organize all of these deliveries.

Both sides reach an agreement through interest-based bargaining.

Collaboration requires you to put yourself in the shoes of the other party. What is important to them? What do they need from you? Why are they offering a specific product or service? Instead of dismissing their offer as different from your needs and therefore unacceptable, you can use collaboration to eval-
58

uate their position and create compromises that will satisfy you and the other party.

Listen

The American Psychological Association (APA) is a scientific organization that specializes in the research of the human mind, body, and condition and endeavors to communicate this information to the world at large. As such, communication plays a huge role in this organization's existence. In fact, the APA has its own special definition for effective communication: the exchange of ideas.

Let's pay special attention, for a moment, to that italicized word: exchange. Communication, in its truest and most effective form, is a transaction. Communication cannot occur if one party is doing all of the talking. Unless there is an exchange of information and ideas, there cannot be an exchange of mutual benefit and value.

This means that even if you read this book cover to cover, employ every tactic and strategy mentioned herein, and practice negotiations night and day, you'll find it very difficult to succeed unless you improve your skills in this third step of the Vanilla Ice Negotiation Strategy: listening.

There are countless reasons why people struggle with listening, especially in a negotiation. You may feel that you need to do most of the talking in order to express your desires and interests more clearly. You might be afraid to listen because you don't want to be subjected to a sales pitch that will convince you to buy things you don't need. You may worry about being trapped or hoodwinked. You might be threatened by the other negotiating party.

Whatever the reason, it's important to recognize the value of listening. Listening allows you to discover opportunities for compromise. Listening provides you with information that may help you save money or get the best service for your buck. Listening can answer your questions and help you discover new questions that you may have.

Those are just the benefits on your side. When you listen during a negotiation, your attitude also has a positive effect on the other party. Listening can disarm a wedding service provider who is harsh or confrontational. Listening can communicate your interest and seriousness about working with a service provider. Listening helps the other party feel valued and respected. All of this contributes to a healthier and more productive negotiation environment.

When you listen to the other party, the other party will listen to you. If you want to be heard, start by listening. It's the sharpest negotiation tool in your toolbox. Use it often and well.

Chapter 8
TIPS and TRICKS

The previous chapters in this book have approached the subject of negotiation from several different angles. By learning about the history and culture of negotiation, the personality traits that must be cultivated and nurtured for successful negotiation, and some basic strategies and tenets of profitable negotiation used by the pros, you've already armed yourself with more knowledge and preparedness than most people have when they begin negotiating with wedding service providers and vendors.

Still, there's a virtually infinite pool of knowledge and experience yet to be gained. In this chapter, we'll discuss some tips and tricks that others have used to steer a negotiation toward a successful conclusion. These tips and tricks won't be appropriate in every scenario. You may discover that some of these techniques don't fit your personal style or modus operandi. That's ok. Every single negotiation is different. You may approach one negotiation like a strict business meeting and treat the next like an informal coffee date with a dear friend.

When you negotiate with prospective sellers, you'll be using your best judgment and proceeding as you see fit. There is no script, mathematical equation, or step-by-step pattern that can get you the results you want. Truth be told, you don't even need that. When you embark on a negotiation confidently, calmly, and with a spirit of collaboration, you will very rarely walk away disappointed.

That said, the information in this chapter is designed to stimulate your creative mind, get your gears spinning, and give you an "Aha! I never thought of that! I can definitely use that" kind of moment. Any tool, trick, tactic, or tip can come in handy at a moment's notice.

Contact Past Clients

One of the best ways to show a seller that you are a savvy, professional, streetwise negotiator is to ask for the contact information of past clients. This is a strategy with three distinct benefits.

First, it shows the seller that you're not going to be swayed by talk but by action and evidence. If a seller knows that you're going to contact his or her past clients, that seller is going to get very honest, very fast. The seller knows that you'll be asking about services rendered in the past, the price of those services, the quality of the services, and the overall value. This is the moment where the seller admits any problems he or she has encountered in the past, offers you the truly best possible price, and learns that you mean business.

Second, you'll be able to gain valuable insight into the quality and value of the service or product being sold. You might find, through talking to past customers, that the general satisfaction with the service is severely lacking. You might hear horror story after horror story of agreements that weren't honored, quality that wasn't up to par, or problems encountered after the contract was signed. On the other hand, a conversation with a past customer may reveal the seller to be a phenomenal asset when planning a wedding. Glowing reviews may encourage you to accept compromises, and a good seller knows this.

This brings us to the third benefit of asking for past customer contact information. Granted, a seller isn't at liberty to simply give away the cell phone numbers of past clients. It's likely, however, that some customers have expressed their willingness to act as references on behalf of the seller. You can often gauge the honesty and integrity of a service provider simply by watching how he or she reacts to the request for customer opinions.

"Of course, I have a list of clients you can contact" or "Yes, let me get my feedback forms and show you what my clients have to say" is a good sign. "We don't provide that information" or "We don't collect feedback from our clients" is a warning sign.

A Word of Caution

There are many helpful websites that give customers an opportunity to review businesses, service providers, and vendors with whom they have worked in the past. While the information on these sites can be quite enlightening, it's important to remember that there is little to no regulation with regard to who can post. A difficult customer with irrational expectations can create a devastating rant on these review websites, even if the vendor was not at fault. For this reason, it's important to give the seller the opportunity to respond to negative reviews in a negotiation. There's always a second side to every story, and the seller's response to a bad review may eliminate all of your concerns.

The Power of a Handshake

Sometimes, the very simplest actions can have the biggest impact on a negotiation's success potential. This is precisely why small acts of cooperative and congenial behavior, like shaking hands before and after a meeting, possess so much power.

Shaking hands is such a ubiquitous gesture that it seems to have lost all meaning in today's society. And yet, Francesca Gino, an Associate Professor of Business Administration at the Harvard School of Business, has recently completed research that suggests handshaking is more important than we realize.

She states:

> "In the context of a negotiation, a handshake's message can go even further, my research finds... Across many cultures, shaking hands at the beginning and end of a negotiating session conveys a willingness to cooperate and reach a deal that considers the interests of the parties at the table. By paying attention to this behavior, negotiators can communicate their motives and intentions, and better understand how the other side is approaching discussions" (Gino).

This isn't just conjecture or guesswork. Gino and her team completed independent, double-blind studies with groups of negotiators. Half of the groups were instructed to shake hands before and after the negotiation. The other half were given no instructions, and most of these groups didn't shake hands because of time restrictions.

The negotiations bracketed by handshakes were far more successful, collaborative, and productive. As it turns out, a simple handshake is a physical embodiment of all that collaborative strategy we've been discussing.

Just by reaching out and taking the other party's hand, you can show your willingness to cooperate from the get-go.

Never underestimate the power of a firm and congenial handshake.

Capitalize on Business Competition

We live in an increasingly competitive world, and businesses that specialize in wedding-related services or products are feeling that competition more and more acutely. This seems to be especially true for the photography industry. Have you noticed a dramatic boom in the photography industry over the past five years? Because this business requires very little investment capital (a high quality camera, photo editing software, and a basic website are really all that's required to get a business off the ground), professional photography is one of the fastest-growing online-based businesses in the world.

That competition can be found in just about any business in today's tough market. That's good news for you, the buyer, and you can use this information to increase your negotiation potential. While it's never a good idea to "threaten" the other party in a negotiation by suggesting you'll simply give your services to a competitor, there are healthy and productive ways to use competitor information in a negotiation.

For example, let's continue with the photography illustration. You can access other photography websites or call other companies before negotiating with your top choice. Ask questions during the negotiation about differences in wedding photography packages, pricing, options, and photography styles between the photography company you are negotiating with and some of its competitors. These answers will likely be very illuminating. You'll learn more about the business in question, understand why pricing differences occur, and immediately know whether or not you want to work with a particular company.

Get it in Writing: Contract Finalization

Here's an important step of the negotiation process that is often neglected in the beginning: the written agreement. It's important, even with small upstart businesses or talented friends, to get a written contract signed by both parties, especially where money is concerned. Most businesses will have standard contracts available that they use to protect both themselves and you, the client.

Your written agreement should include detailed information about the service being rendered (or the product being sold, depending on the case), an assurance of the quality of that service, information about the price, and details about what happens if you are dissatisfied with the service, if you change your mind about options, if you decide to cancel, etc. A written contract protects you and your investment; don't rely on spoken word agreements.

In addition to the final contract you'll sign with a vendor, it's helpful to take notes during the negotiation and keep a record of points discussed, questions asked and answered, and services described. This is especially valuable if you negotiate in stages, taking time to consider your options before signing on the dotted line. Keeping a sort of negotiation journal will help you recall what was discussed in a previous negotiation, and it will also help you identify key points of strength and weakness in your own negotiation style.

Stop the Presses: Point Out Concerns Before they Snowball

There's a delightful blog post on Marsha Lichtenstein's blog, WomenNegotiate.com, about her personal experience with a trouble-filled contract. In Marsha's case, this troublesome contract involved home remodeling and repairs. Much to her chagrin, she discovered that a critical step was missed during the process of building new walls in her home. To remedy the problem, she immediately called the contractor, mentioned the issue, and asked for ways the problem could be corrected. The contractor agreed to a meeting and the issue was settled.

If she had simply skipped this step, she would have avoided an awkward conversation and the potential for stress that comes from additional negotiation. She was probably tempted to do just that, and avoidance of confrontation is something that many women deal with on a regular basis. However, the final product she would have received (incorrectly built and designed walls) would have been more frustrating than the post-negotiation conversation. By addressing the issue immediately before the problem had a chance to snowball, headaches were avoided and Marsha got what she required from her contractor.

Negotiations don't stop when the work begins. You may find yourself negotiating up until the point where you walk down the aisle to meet your beloved. The trick is to address concerns immediately rather than putting them off or avoiding them altogether. Sellers want to satisfy their clients. Point out problems as soon as they occur and you will provide the seller with an opportunity to satisfy you. They'll appreciate it, especially if you thank them and give them a great review for addressing your concerns.

Must Haves, Really Wants, and Plan B's

Let's be honest: this is your wedding, and you want it to be perfect. No one is blaming you for that. Your wedding is an incredibly special and significant day, and it's a day you've probably been dreaming about for at least a couple of decades. You're entitled to a long wish list, and no one expects you to take compromise or shattered dreams lightly.

Now, let's be real: it's highly unlikely that your wedding will materialize in exactly the way you dreamed it. When you were five, you may have really wanted to get married in a rainbow sherbet castle, surrounded by unicorns and adorned with glittering fairy dust. That's just an example. Your dream wedding probably looks a little different than that. The point is this: sometimes our wishes can't become reality, and sometimes they can. It's important to make the distinction and prepare to compromise.

Some people mistakenly believe that approaching a negotiation with a Plan B immediately weakens their bargaining position. This is completely opposite from the truth! Instead of weakening your position, having a Plan B in place loosens you up, allows you to accommodate the unexpected, and increases your chances of finding success and satisfaction.

In Ask For It, Babcock and Laschever refer to the Plan B as a "BATNA." This stands for the "Best Alternative to a Negotiated Agreement." If you cannot get what you want, what is the best second option available to you? Maybe you're willing to accept a higher price. Maybe you can adjust your expectations a little bit. Or maybe you know of another service provider who can correct a mistake made by the originally contracted party.

Marsha Lichtenstein had a BATNA in her house-remodeling fiasco scenario. If the contractor wasn't willing or able to correct the mistake, Lichtenstein was perfectly willing to cancel the contract, pay for the work already completed, and look elsewhere to get the job finished. Using this BATNA as a backup, though, Lichtenstein was able to convince the contractor to correct the error. A Plan B can be an invaluable negotiation

68

tool, and it's important to have one.

It is often helpful for engaged couples to organize their desires into two separate categories: Must Haves and Really Wants. Your list of Must Haves will include everything on which you are unwilling to compromise. Maybe you absolutely want to be married in a specific location. Maybe your cake simply has to have three tiers. Maybe your bridesmaids' dresses need to be the perfect shade of plum. There's no rule as to what falls in this category, but these should be the absolutes, the aspects of your wedding for which you aren't willing to budge. Understand, of course, that a longer list of Must Haves makes for a more difficult negotiation journey.

Your list of Really Wants comes with a list of Plan B's. Write out the things you really want to see in your wedding. Next to each Really Want, include an option that would work for you if that particular item is unachievable. Here's an example list:

- Wedding Cake: White cake with Champagne frosting, if Champagne is unavailable will accept Almond or Vanilla flavoring.
- Entertainment: Jazz Band to play at the reception, if Jazz Band is unavailable will accept jazz combo or DJ who plays 1940s standards.
- Bridesmaid Dresses: Plum colored dresses from favorite designer, if these are too expensive or unavailable will accept plum colored dresses in a modern, attractive style.

As you can see from this list, the desires are clearly expressed and quite detailed. However, the writer of this list has included secondary options that might be a little bit easier or more affordable to secure. In some cases, like the plum-colored bridesmaid dresses, creating this list reveals true priorities. The color of the dress in the example above is obviously more important than the manufacturer or designer. Feel free to use the worksheets at the end of this book to help you organize a

Must Have/Really Want list.

Chapter 9
PRACTICE MAKES PERFECT

Negotiating contracts for a wedding is just one of those things that seem to invite butterflies to permanently nest in our stomachs and encourage our sweat glands to crank it into overdrive. There's nothing wrong with feeling nervous about a negotiation, but excessive nervousness or fear can get in the way of successful communication during a negotiation.

If your nervousness is impeding your ability to communicate clearly and effectively, preventing you from responding successfully to confrontational situations, or causing you to avoid negotiation altogether, you might just need a little practice.

Working as a couple is a great way to counteract negotiation nervousness and become professionals at negotiation. In this chapter, you'll find six different negotiation scenarios that can act as prompts for a little negotiation role-play. Role-playing negotiation can take some of the edge off that nervous. Take turns with a partner acting out the negotiation. By playing the part of the seller, you can begin to understand what the other party wants or needs in the negotiation. By playing the part of the buyer, you'll be able to anticipate questions, scenarios, and tactics used by the seller.

You can use these role-play prompts for any type of negotiation. Whether you are negotiating the purchase of a cake, the rental of a tuxedo, or the use of a church, going through these six prompts will ensure you are well-prepared for the conversation.

Prompt #1:

Begin by practicing clear communication of your interests, desires, and needs to the other party. Gather all of the facts, use websites or photographs to reference services you like, provide details, list concerns, etc. At the end of this prompt, ask your partner if he or she feels like you effectively communicated your needs. Practice until you've communicated as briefly and clearly as possible.

Prompt #2:

Next, use collaboration and listening skills to understand the interests, rather than the positions, of the other party. Initiate a conversation that will ensure that both of your interests have been expressed and heard. Try to find a compromise that will create a win/win situation rather than a win/lose situation.

Prompt #3:

In this scenario, have the person playing the seller adopt a negative behavior like a confrontational attitude, dismissiveness, belligerence, etc. Use the skills you've researched and developed to respond to this negative behavior and redirect it. Example: A bride-to-be shows her dream wedding cake to a potential baker, but the baker immediately points out everything wrong and impractical with the cake, rather than discussing options.

Prompt #4:

In this scenario, have the person playing the seller adopt excessively pushy selling tactics. Practice fielding these hard sell tactics, continuing to express your own interests, and avoiding purchasing services that you don't want or need. Example: A bride-to-be wants to rent a simple car for transportation from the church to the reception site. The vehicle rental agent, however, wants the bride to purchase stretch limousines, horse-drawn carriages, trained dragons, or some other excessive purchase that exceeds her budget limitations.

Prompt #5:

Practice giving a firm "no" during the negotiation. Have the person playing the seller do everything in his or her power to keep the conversation going. Your responsibility is to clearly, politely, and firmly exit the negotiation without paying for unwanted services.

Prompt #6:

In this situation, practice asking for time to consider the offer. The person playing the seller should offer incentives for signing a contract immediately. Example: An amazing 10% discount can be applied to the contract, but only if the buyer signs immediately. In this situation, the buyer should try to explain why he or she wants time to consider the offer while still showing interest and commitment to the negotiation and the contract.

As you encounter different negotiation situations, you may be able to identify areas of weakness. You can create your own prompts and role-play situations to work on these negotiation deficiencies. Additionally, if you approach negotiation as a couple rather than an individual, you may find that you have comparable strengths and weaknesses, and you can rely on one another to present the strongest possible position in a negotiation.

READY. SET. GO.

If you're going to plan a wedding, you are going to negotiate. There is no easy way around it. You could accept every price given to you, nod in silence as vendors describe their products and services, and keep your lips mashed together even when problems arise.

You're still negotiating.

Instead of treating negotiation like a terrifying obstacle that must be crossed, view your wedding planning process as an opportunity for growth and development. You'll learn more about yourself, your desires, your strengths, and your weaknesses than you ever thought possible. The skills you develop when you start negotiating wedding contracts will be invaluable to you throughout the rest of your life.

Good negotiation starts with self-reflection. Developing a healthy sense of self-worth moves you closer to the finish line.

Adequate preparation, healthy communication, approaching the negotiation as a collaboration rather than a conflict, developing alternatives or "BATNAs" to your desires, and learning how to deal with troublesome individuals are all secondary to that one, important first step.

You are capable of negotiating anything. If you are passionate about the subject, confident in yourself, and convinced that you are valuable and that your opinions are worthy of expression and consideration, you *will* succeed.

Believe in yourself and your ability. *Navigating the tricky waters of negotiation really is that simple.*

NEGOTIATION WORKSHEET

Download for Free at
www.WeddingPlanningFun.com/NegotiationSheets

Wedding Service (Example: Photographer):

_____

Ideal Budget: _____   **Maximum Budget:** _____

Must Haves:

Really Wants:

Alternative Options (BATNA):

Notes:

NEGOTIATION WORKSHEET

Download for Free at
www.WeddingPlanningFun.com/NegotiationSheets

Wedding Service (Example: Photographer):

_____

Ideal Budget: _____   **Maximum Budget:** _____

Must Haves:

Really Wants:

Alternative Options (BATNA):

Notes:

DON'T FORGET...

If you're planning a wedding, don't forget to check out the other titles in Sue Shafer's Wedding Planning series, including...

Wedding
p l a n n i n g
Ask These Questions
to avoid
Costly and Upsetting
Problems

Sue Shafer's first book in the Wedding Planning series walks soon-to-be-wed couples through the most common wedding services, providing lists of valuable questions to ask photographers, caterers, wedding planners, rental companies, musicians, and more!

Available at Amazon.com or WeddingPlanningFun.com

PLEASE HELP...

Word-of-mouth is crucial for any author to succeed. If you enjoyed the book, please consider leaving a review at Amazon, even if it is only a line or two; it would make all the difference and would be very much appreciated.

RESOURCES

For further reading, valuable information about negotiations both in the workplace and in other life situations, and additional studies, research, and advice, be sure to check out the following websites and books. Many of these resources were referenced in this book.

www.WeddingPlanningFun.com

www.WomenNegotiate.com

www.IrenaOBrien.com

www.SimpliLearn.com

Babcock, Linda, and Sara Laschever. *Ask for It: How Women Can Use the Power of Negotiation to Get What They Really Want.* New York: Bantam Dell, 2008. Kindle AZW File.

Babcock, Linda, and Sara Laschever. W*omen Don't Ask: The High Cost of Avoiding Negotiation-- and Positive Strategies for Change.* New York: Bantam, 2007. Print.

Brzezinski, Mika. *Knowing Your Value: Women, Money, and Getting What You're Worth.* New York: Weinstein, 2011. Print.

Gino, Francesca. "To Negotiate Effectively, First Shake Hands." Harvard Business Review. HBR.org, 4 June 2014. Web. 05 June 2014.

Hawkins, David R. *Letting Go: The Pathway of Surrender.* W. Sedona, AZ: Veritas, 2012. Print.

ACKNOWLEDGMENTS

I would like to thank Dr. Marsha Lichtenstein (WomenNegotiate.com) for reviewing the manuscript and writing the Foreword to this book.

I would also like to thank book cover designer, graphic designer, illustrator, and editor Travis Wisely for his creativity and doggedness to get it right. Travis is also my partner in bringing children's story character FantasticalFred.com to life.

Finally, I wish to thank Ron, my partner and editor, for his untiring efforts, valuable suggestions, and vast improvements to this book and many other projects.

DEDICATION

This book is dedicated to three once-tween girls Allegra, Gabrielle, and Giuliana who embraced the idea of negotiation at an early age on a dance trip to New York City. Remembering how they heaped praise on me when I negotiated the price of a purse still makes me smile.

ABOUT the AUTHOR

Sue Shafer is an award winning scholarly writer for her work on the Paradox of Intention and has edited two Canadian Health Care Management texts. She has a love of research and writing and has traditionally taken on projects in health and business. Through her career as a CEO of national non-profits and charities, she has been responsible for planning many events and has negotiated many contracts.

Sue coaches high achieving women, both entrepreneurs and those with careers. She started this book project because through her research and experience she recognized that women do have difficulty negotiating. She started this book to help women who are planning their weddings, but her research uncovered that men also can use a hand in becoming better negotiators. Her desire is to help couples save money, reduce stress, and have the wedding they desire by being able to better negotiate their wedding contracts.

For fun Sue has also created, with illustrator Travis Wisely, Fantastical Fred and The Case Of The Missing Smile. The children's story is based on the life of Frederic Artemis Dylan her dog nephew who was smart, a diva, a clown, and a little sneaky. You can find Fred on his website:

www.FantasticalFred.com

Sue loves reading and is an insatiable learner; she loves animals, salsa dancing, and the Ottawa Senators hockey team. Sue lives with her husband, Ron, in Albany, New York.

COPYRIGHT